THE WIT

TWENTY-20

STORIES AND LESSONS FROM THE PANDEMIC YEAR

Curated by Tope Akintayo

Twenty-20: Stories and Lessons from the Pandemic Year

Copyright © 2020: Albarka Wakili, Avwemoya Izoduwa Ogheneochuko, Basit Jamiu, Oluwabukunmi Familoye, Busayo Oyewole, Eniola Oluwafolakemi Olatoye, Haneefah AbdulRahman, Ibrahim Babátúndé Ibrahim, Lawretta Egba, Osatare Omonkhegbe, R'Jay, Tobi Eyinade, Zainab Muhammed.

ISBN: 979-858-34924-2-8

All rights reserved. No part of this book may be used or reproduced in any manner whatsoever without written permission except in the case of brief quotations embodied in critical articles or reviews.

Published as part of *The Witsprouts Project,* by The Moveee Co.

Curated by Tope Akintayo & Edited by Basit Jamiu

Design and Formatting by Tope Akintayo

This page intentionally left blank.

CURATOR'S NOTE
Tope Akintayo

For humankind, 2020 was an unexpected bully. It took advantage of human limits and weaknesses, boxing us up, driving us crazy, killing us softly, and pushing us beyond the expected limits.

No year is without its troubles but 2020 opened a newer kind of pain, a newer sense of loss, an unprecedented disruption of plans. This year however is not without its collateral beauty.

Epictetus, an ancient philosopher taught that, in the end, what happens to mankind does not matter, what matters is how mankind reacts to what happens. We all reacted to the year in different ways: the pessimist amongst us complained about the wind that blew throughout the year; the optimist expected the wind to stop or become calmer; the realist proactively attempted to adjust the sails.

The ending of a year like this is just a beginning, with all the memories and wisdom it instilled in us. Therefore, as it is, the year remains with us eternally, in unique ways; in different versions.

This project was created as a little record of voices, reflections and experiences. Fourteen contributors from different professions, at different stages of life and with unique experiences share their personal story and perspective on the pandemic year.

With amazing contributions from Albarka Wakili, Avwemoya Izoduwa Ogheneochuko, Basit Jamiu, Oluwabukunmi Familoye, Busayo Oyewole, Eniola Oluwafolakemi Olatoye, Haneefah AbdulRahman, Ibrahim Babátúndé Ibrahim, Lawretta Egba, Osatare Omonkhegbe, R'Jay, Tobi Eyinade, Zainab Muhammed, you are sure to have an enjoyable read.

I appreciate support received from individuals who threw in effort to ensure the success of this project. Basit Jamiu, for taking time to rework the draft into an enjoyable piece. Also, contributions from Anna Suberu, Timi Odueso, Omoya Simult, Maryam Hussain and Ganiyat Sani.

The goal is to prompt everyone to look beyond the pains of the year into collateral beauties. The hope is that every person finds peace with the way the year hits them and forges ahead in all the little different ways they are able to. The mission is to inspire a heart of gratitude for all the wisdom and memories that the year leaves behind in our minds. To face the year ahead, we must all embrace optimism and courage but above all, gratitude for the simple pleasures of life.

TABLE OF CONTENTS

Curator's Note
The Pandemic Culture
   Avwemoya Izoduwa Ogheneochuko..................1
Revived Intimacy
   Haneefah AbdulRahman................................. 6
Just a Girl Asking to be Loved
   Busayo Oyewole..12
Down, Not Out
   Ibrahim Babátúndé Ibrahim 15
Beyond the Storm
   Lawretta Egba.. 23
Mi Said Life is Fickle
   Basit Jamiu.. 28
Of Highs and Lows
   Tobi Eyinade...31
A Lockdown Hero
   Albarka Wakili 34
COVID-19 and Me
   Zainab Muhammed.. 39
Only When You Speak Up
   Osatare Omonkhegbe 42
High Hopes
   Oluwabukunmi Familoye................................ 46
No One Knows
   R'Jay 50
Dear Diary
   Eniola Oluwafolakemi Olatoye 55
Contributors' Note

x

THE PANDEMIC CULTURE
Avwemoya Izoduwa Ogheneochuko

Sometimes, looking at the world move like a running stream, I wonder what the first trimester was like for me. When the news came that we had to travel back home due to the scary surge of the virus. With the daily deaths and rapid spread, I felt my fear rise each day.

Amidst all of the confusion, mixed emotions and quest for safety, I called my father, asked him to send me money, so I'd stay back in school. I feared boarding a bus back to warri, seeing as its chances of me contacting the virus was higher. Long story short, home was my next stop; Nigerian parents and selective deafness.

Albeit, that from a pandemic, we learned intentional communication. It became a tradition, for friends, waking up to each other's chirps and singing ourselves to sleep. A culture that kept death at bay.

Realizing that COVID-19 had a Nigerian version and that this version had fraud in its DNA woke everybody up.

Somewhere in the midst of all of this, we started asking questions, "What are we doing?", "When all of this is over, what will we say we achieved?"

As much as I tried to convince myself that in the end, making it out alive was enough achievement, it still felt insufficient. Adequate but not sufficient, so the hustle began; staying safe and making money.

Being an ambivert, it was hard to pick a struggle. Watching my brother make money that period didn't help, while my heart bubbled with joy for the success he was achieving in his endeavours, I felt hollow. All he did was work with a laptop, teach kids on Google and run some codes, while I was there in the same house but with a shit load of empty pockets, working on books that may never get published. In that space of time, it dawned on me, that my mental health was at the receiving end of all the negativity and that I had to choose staying sane over staying safe and making money. The pressure from friends and the social media wasn't helping, so I took time off. For a month, I stayed away from the internet, I was reading, writing, meditating and most importantly, I was healing. I learnt to be happy for my brother without necessarily feeling like a box of nonsense myself, and in my happy hour, life threw me her favorite line: good things don't last forever.

In the twinkle of an eye, sadness paid us a visit. My father's health deteriorated. This once, I feared we'd lose him. The only way I could express how I felt that time was through a poem:

> *There was a time when*
> *mouths couldn't talk*
> *a time I lived, at the*
> *mercy of uncertainty*
> *a time when love did all*
> *the talking*
>
> *I had seen her, love, from*
> *my mother's eyes, the*
> *tears she fought to hide*
> *and the strength she*
> *showed, for no one had*
> *ever seen the hero fall.*
>
> *There was a time when*
> *mouths could not talk*
> *and signs were the next*
> *language*
> *love taught us to adjust,*

*to learn new languages
to compromise, love
taught us.*

*There was a time when
mouths couldn't talk
for her opening would be
life's closure
a time I existed
a time still fresh in my
memory
a time when all the
stories I had for papa
turned to tears and
aching head
a time I was afraid to
close my eyes
'cause no one knew what
darkness would bring
for she was hardly a
carrier of good news.*

*A time I was free to do all
but breakdown
for if I gave in to the ache
of my heart
black roses would sprout
without repentance*

*and we all know black
has history.*

*There was a time when
mouths couldn't talk
a time I cried behind
closed doors
a time I died and
resurrection wasn't an option."*

Seeing papa get well was all the miracle I needed for 2020. This time, I learned to see. To see the things I needed to see, things I had failed to see in my quest for an essence that was right before me, and if there is one thing I truly realized, it's that a grateful heart indeed is a good medicine.

Sometimes, all we really need to do is block out the noise, dead the pressure, appreciate the little things, sip a glass of juice and move.

REVIVED INTIMACY
Haneefah AbdulRahman

The woman raised her hand and I quickly turned my face away, to the right. I thought she was going to hit me for removing her child's hands from my thigh. I thought so because she was wearing a scowl. I was wrong; she raised her hand to adjust her scarf which had sloped down to the back of her neck. She hadn't said a word since we left Zaria.

Her elder daughter signalled to her to see a place which seemed as though they knew when we got to Jaji and she smiled. The woman smiled for the first time since we started our journey to Kaduna.

Her baby's little hands were cute, but they irritated me. I couldn't stand to look at her. The child was all over me, crawling like a slug, poking fingers into my nose, reaching for my ears.

It was the first time, after months of confinement, days of reflection, that I went out, travelled for a few hours on road. I had to go to Zaria to get some important documents I had left in my hostel, gathering dust, for months.

The Pandemic made me scared of everyone, and there I was, sitting in the back seat with three other people. It was hell enough and I can hardly put the facemask on for more than ten minutes - it had always felt like a strong hand trying to suffocate me.

"Conductor, four people no too much for back?" I had asked when I was about to board the bus.

"Aunty, you go enter abi make I carry another person? People dey wey go gree enter boot oh," The bus conductor had replied. His rudeness reeked for miles.

I had no choice but to squeeze in.

I thought of home as the bus moved - the lockdown had made so many people look back to analyze their past and see what they can do with their present. I thought of hope and hopelessness that flickered on people's faces. I thought of how dry Ramadan was and how scared we were to pray in congregation; we couldn't even do the exchange of food we usually do in Ramadan.

The pandemic had turned a lot of people into a ruined house. Most people would say it brought no single fortune. But for me it was in between.

When the lockdown was announced, I had arrived home from school, my family was really excited to see me for I seldom came home from school even during holidays - I was always busy. At some point, they thought I was shutting them out until I explained to them how demanding my course of study is.

It was exciting to have everyone at home, the house was full: my elder sister, the four boys, Dad and Mum. We would watch movies together and talk about it the next day. We are crazy about movies in my house. Dad would challenge the ladies in the house once in a while, "Daddy is going to prepare a very delicious meal. Just watch. You ladies only brag, but you know I cook better than any of you." He wouldn't even allow us to help him out with anything while he cooked. So, we just watched TV while he cooked.

Honestly, Dad is a good cook, but I can't say he cooks better than any of us; my mum, sister or me.

The lockdown gave the blessings of filling in the closeness that was missing. For months, I had not been able to spend good family time with Dad and my immediate younger brother especially. Those two are the closest to me in my family.

I knew Dad was going through a lot. One evening, he was seated outside while we were all in the living room. I decided to join him when he didn't come into the house after some hours. I sat on the bench with him, he was so concentrated on the sky. "How have you been?" He had asked, still staring at the sky.

"I have been OK, Daddy," I said. "How have you been?"

"I have been fine," He had said with uncertainty. He knew that I knew he wasn't saying everything.

"Tell me about everything, Daddy. You have become thinner than the last time I saw you," I had said.

That night we talked about so many things. Who said talking isn't a good therapy? I couldn't solve almost anything, yet I saw sparks of relief inside of my father after we spoke that night about our challenges. I could see through him.

"I am tired of staying at home and now the pandemic," My immediate younger brother said while we were taking a walk one morning.

"Don't worry. Everything happens for a reason," I had said to him. I had no right to think I could make him feel better.

Somehow, I felt I had failed him. He had applied for NDA twice and he wasn't shortlisted. On many nights he would leave the house without a word of where he was going, and when he came back, he would sit outside for hours before coming in. I had tried so many times to make him pour his heart out to me, but it was always so hard. My courage kept running away whenever I needed it.

My sister, on the other hand, kept mumbling and complaining about NYSC's refusal to overlook the pandemic and invite them.

Remembering some of the memories while staying with my family during the lockdown made me chuckle, forgetting I was in a tight bus. I felt a little bit embarrassed. I felt the baby's little hand on my skin again, this time she touched my hand and somehow, I didn't see any fault in her. I took her hand into mine and smiled at her.

Life is a risk, anyway. When I looked up at her mother, she was smiling at me. The woman was trying to say something with her hands, that was when I realized that she was dumb. I nodded even though I didn't know what she was saying. We arrived at Kawo and the woman waved me goodbye when we alighted from the bus and parted ways.

JUST A GIRL ASKING TO BE LOVED
Busayo Oyewole

Before 2020 I was pretty secure in who I was, I think. Maybe a little avoidant here and there, but who isn't?

There's this attachment theory in the field of psychology that proposes that people handle adult relationships by how well attached they were as kids to their primary caregivers. In essence, it asks, did your primary caregiver fuck you up or not?

Mary Ainsworth, a developmental psychologist says, if you were not fucked up as a child and you had a steady kind of upbringing with steady love that wasn't conditional or flaky, you grow up to be a secure adult. An independent, confident adult, comfortable with intimacy, who ends up in a perfect secure relationship. *One can only hope.*

But if you were fucked up, one way or the other, either by promises not met, or parents that weren't present (the list is endless), you end up developing an 'avoidant' or an 'anxious' attachment style. I don't have to spell it out, that these two are not good. The avoidants avoid intimacy, they are the kind of people who just can't handle adult relationships, people who turn on their heels at the faintest echo of commitment. And there's the anxious folks, the ones who want assurances, the clingy ones, the ones that want to move in after 3 dates - I hate them, the millennial dating folklore hates them, we all hate them (although I'm beginning to think they get a bad reputation).

I'm writing this because, in 2020, I find myself in need of assurances - clingy - I've become something I despise. I find myself asking for love where there's none. But like a proper student of psychology, I've been psychoanalysing myself, asking, what is it about 2020 that makes me wanna hurdle in a corner and cry, and fling myself at my lover and ask to be loved completely or not at all?

Is it this unprecedented lockdown manifesting these unprecedented symptoms? Is it the many months of imposed solitude that has diffused into this wretched loneliness? What about 2020 has revealed this fatal flaw? What is this mirror of a 2020 that has forced me to look, really look and see this person that I do not recognise?

Has she been there this whole time? this anxiously-attached girl, and according to Mary Ainsworth, obviously fucked up. I find myself asking, will 2021 bring a new normal or perhaps an old familiar one. Or has 2020 revealed the true me - this broken soul, with a broken attachment style, asking to be loved.

***

But today I'm without a lover and I'm not begging to be loved. Instead, I'm looking outside my window, watching the trees shed their leaves. It's autumn and 2020 will soon run out. I'm eager for 2020 to go, but not these beautiful leaves. These yellow-orange leaves, shimmering and fighting against the wind, holding on for as long as they can.

I'm wondering why they have to fall. It seems so cruel for such beautiful things to fall and leave the trees vulnerable.

A quick Google search tells me that the trees shed their leaves to survive the harshness of winter. By making themselves vulnerable, they save themselves. They shed their leaves knowing, this too will pass, and next year they can grow greener, steadier, and more secure leaves. (One can only hope.)

DOWN, NOT OUT
Ibrahim Babátúndé Ibrahim

The harmattan is harsh. I'm wearing a pair of socks over another pair of socks, and a thermal coat over two t-shirts. The air is dry, seeming to clutch and squeeze whatever it touches. My nose is only just healing from its grip and I'm learning not to move my mouth too much when I speak so as not to split my flaking lips. This reality is lost to me, however, as my fingers hit away at my computer's keypad. It takes an uneven chorus of the birthday song to draw me from the words on my screen back to my table in the study.

I had been paying attention to the clock but didn't realize when the long arm arrived at twelve. This is partly due to the silence of my phone. It sits quietly across the table; no ding, no vibration, no screen coming alive. Other years, it would be buzzing from many hours before the dot of twelve. People made time at crossover services just to step aside and wish me a happy birthday. My special day was a big deal. Well, the day is still the first day of January, perhaps it's something about the celebrant that has changed.

"How old are you now? How old are you now? How old are you now (baby) (uncle Ibrahim)? How old are you now?"

As my love, Adunni and her sister, Aisha round up the third stanza of the birthday song in their uncoordinated but joy-ridden rendition, I soak in all the love and adoration their voices, big smiles, and song-sways are exuding, standing up to clasp them into a tight embrace. This means so much to me, but I'm reminded of how clear it is that so much has indeed changed about me.

I'm no longer 'Skillz', the successful media and entertainment consultant; former channel manager of a TV station and general manager of a foremost record label. My social media handles no longer have the glitz, and generally, social relevance is no longer my strongpoint. I traded it all in when I decided to walk away from a decade-old career to pursue writing; worst still, when I waved bye-bye to single life, pitching my tent with Adunni and withdrawing to a low profile.

"Your phone hasn't rung?" Adunni asked, leading me to our room.

I shook my head.

"You're starting all over again, baby. You're at the bottom now. Your talent will shine through and all that seems lost will come back," She says all these in a hushed tone so as not to wake our baby. Then she takes my other hand and starts to pray for me.

Well, there are no regrets, but it sometimes stings when I think about how fast things can change, and how everything moves on without you like you were never there. Leaving means I left a source of livelihood behind. Writing has always come naturally to me, but so far, it's not showing any signs of yielding desired fruits. This family right here and the indescribable love that binds it is all that has kept me.

Though a cloud of gloom looms over my subconscious, I know there's still so much to be excited about. Yes, it's been ten months since I've been submitting my work; ten months since I've been dealing with rejections, but one of my stories is finally getting published this January. Adunni is heavy with our second child. We finally left the chaos of Lagos and the torment of landlords for the peace and serenity of Ilorin, in a big compound that is all ours.

There's a faint knock on the door, interrupting my thoughts and Adunni's prayers. She pauses, then asks, "what is it, Aisha?"

"Uncle Ibrahim's phone is vibrating."

Adunni's eyes find mine. I see a glint of excitement in them.

"Who is it?" I ask.

"It's your mum."

Like a burning candle lighting up a dead one, my eyes take some glint off Adunni's and my face breaks into a smile.

The TV is tuned to CNN, the interface bright and beautiful, but the on-screen text bearing bad news after bad news. Two days ago, on New Year's Day, it was news of Jakarta floods. The day after, a plane crash in Sudan killed eighteen people. Earlier today, the news broke of the USA striking and killing an Iranian general. As the story is developing, I'm scrolling through Twitter trend-table to see 'World War III' trending at number 1 worldwide.

"I hope Trump does not plunge the world into war this year o. His appetite is becoming too big for his own good," I say to Adunni who is just walking into the room.

She settles on the sofa, stretches out her legs, rubs her baby bump, then says, "if you're paying any attention to this virus in China, you'll see that you're focusing on the wrong war. If this virus should make it out of there ehn, it will show humanity pepper."

A light wind rolls waste paper and biscuit foils along the tarred ground as I pace up and down a deserted corridor. It's May and I'm a block away from the maternity ward at the Ilorin General Hospital, where Adunni is surely screaming her head off, nudged on by the doctor and his midwives. There's so much that's scary about that. The uncertainties of childbirth are there , but the biggest causes of worry are all Coronavirus-related.

The virus did make it out of China and in fact seeped across the world like wildfire on a fuel-doused field. Airport checks could not stop it. It incubated in the lungs of travelers where even the carrier was oblivious to its presence. By March when borders began to fall shut like dominoes across all countries, the virus already assumed the dictator role, filling up the morgues beyond capacity, forcing everyone to stay at home, and pretty much grinding everything, everywhere to a halt.

A window across the corridor stares my reflection back at me. The hair around my head and face have grown out of control, much like a lion's mane, sprouting from all sides of the face mask I have around my chin. Sweat seeps from my pores, wetting the mask at the edges. I lean forward for a closer look, seeing different emotions struggle for space in my reddened, tired eyes. I am as excited as I am anxious. The love of my life is doing the delivery thing alone, pushing a child into the world in the thick of a pandemic!

"Mr. Ibrahim!"

It must be by the third call before I break from my trance. I run towards the direction of the voice and ask its owner, "how's she?"

"She just delivered a baby boy. Congratulations!"

"Baby, can you find out how many people this thing has killed in Nigeria? I need the figure for this piece I'm working on," I tell Adunni. She's with me in the study, sitting on a rocking chair placed directly before the standing fan. Her face is glued to her phone while our son clutches and sucks on her breast.

I already peeled my clothes down to singlets and briefs. The heat is menacing and I'm getting nothing from the fan, so I pull away the singlet too.

She chuckles and says, "sorry," before her face straightens into a frown. "The statistics from yesterday says eight hundred plus."

I breathe a heavy sigh.

"Do you see how they're just numbers; statistics?" she says, her voice cocooned in sadness. "These are real people, but their names don't even matter anymore."

This is so true it shifts a wave of guilt through my body. My mind floats back to the first day of the year when my phone not ringing had me feeling down. Even then, I was much more than mere statistics. I was a person at a transition point in his life, living, breathing, blessed with the luxury of having problems, and the privilege of starting afresh.

My family has grown bigger with the gift of yet another child; a beautiful boy. Following my drought of 2019, publications have poured in every other month since the turn of January, dispersing my words far and wide. I have built new relationships that are more meaningful. My reality is different and I'm a lot happier. All these are much more than the dead can wish for. I realize that even though it is human to feel down, I should learn to be more grateful as long as I'm breathing, because being down and being out are really not the same thing.

BEYOND THE STORM
Lawretta Egba

Albert Einstein once said that time is only "a stubbornly persistent illusion."

While there are many ways to interpret the illusion of time, one can rightly say that it doesn't matter what year it is or whether it counts as the past, present, or future, there will always be darkness as much as light.

The real world simply does not rest on the back of happy endings and plans don't always work out in the same way they were inked. 2020 was not the first year a pandemic happened. It also wasn't the first time that violence ensued following mass protests or the first time that good people died. Yet, the year 2020 was a different kind of madness; everything became amplified in 2020. There was just something awfully debilitating about the year – and every single one of us, across genders, race, or age – felt it. Humankind probably did not know it could take this much before this year.

For one, the pandemic was a major spanner in the wheel crippling economies, taking jobs, and taking lives. The violence and massacre that ensued in Nigeria with the End SARS protests, the mass murder of civilians also following police brutality in Uganda, and even the resurfacing of the black lives matter campaign in the United States, are just some of the different smaller pandemics we had to deal with.

For the first time ever, the world was indeed united with common goals and common enemies. We watched the same news, used the same social applications, and made our plight known globally through similar hashtags. Unprecedented as it was, for the first time, we all paused. For a world that was constantly on the run and in motion, 2020 made us halt and this shift in our psyche just happens to be the very thing that will nudge us into the morning after.

Across the world and across economies, many experienced a massive shift in what they projected the year to be and how it eventually turned out. However, unlike most people, 2020 was not nearly as bad – at least as far as the general challenges go. For some reason, it birthed a different kind of luck for me.

While others were losing jobs, I had more jobs than I could handle and had to carry some of the biggest and fastest business expansions ever. As far as business, finance, and career were concerned, I was one of the lucky ones. But in spite of the luck on the career front, 2020 was simply not the kind of year that left anyone whole. In other words, believing that you survived 2020 unscathed is tantamount to believing the sun is shining in the dark of night. And while you can recover from financial setbacks, mental and psychological impacts are much harder to shake off.

Like many people, I too had a higher sense of optimism with the year 2020. However, the year tapered down like a wide grin that folded into sadness and ultimately indifference. At different points over the course of the year, I wanted to run. I found myself constantly searching for an escape. Spirituality was also on an all-time low. Worse off, I lost faith in all the things I couldn't control – things like pandemics, death, and even societal change. For the first time in my life, I considered running away into a different reality. But just as we find amazing opportunities in the midst of seemingly daunting challenges, the madness of the year 2020 birthed a myriad of lessons and many of them, I will indeed cherish forever.

The first is the need for strong communities of friends and families. With the world forced to shut down, I was reminded of the power of close ties with loved ones. Things may not be perfect, but having people to weather the storm with you makes all the difference. The next thing I learnt is that nobody really knows what the future holds, so be willing to adapt. The strides I experienced in my career were in no way like the plans I had written down. 2020 taught us the need to grow *in spite of*.

I also learnt that freedom is a thing of the mind. The year 2020 constrained us at different points physically, mentally, and psychologically in more ways than one. True emancipation starts from your mind and ultimately transcends all that exists around you. Until you believe you are free, the world will always find a way to beat you down. As far as my physical appearance and health go, the year ceded many of us unsolicited additional pounds. From someone who will ordinarily never let herself go, the 7kg heavier version of me can tell you that it is okay to let yourself go sometimes. On a general note, 2020 taught us never to stop moving. You can take breaks, but do not stop. Live in the moment, and love freely.

Finally, do not underestimate the power of the 'virtual world' – as some still call it. Social media and the digital world in general shaped many of the activities of the year. Geographical location is no longer a barrier. There is so much that can be done with the tools that are available to us in terms of willing change and creating better paths for ourselves. The internet is the future and 2020 made that a little clearer. But as much as we love it, we must still fear it because sometimes our greatest strengths too can be our greatest weaknesses.

MI SAID LIFE IS FICKLE
Basit Jamiu

There was a time I felt that shaking hands as a common culture of greeting will be without modern implication. It was a time when I associated happiness with the cheering excitement of football fans, and my friends talked about 2020 like it was a holy grail. Mi thought the same too only that she had no idea that 2020 would bring so much surprise. Before the pandemic, when Mi was 16, she had wanted to get married in 2020.

Mi is my friend. Someone I consider to be a conversation buddy. She is vivacious and laughs like a baby. Like Mi, I was staying in Keffi when the first wave of the virus communicated its presence. There was fear but there was also hope. In Keffi, Mi had a few months to complete her National Youth Service and I was pursuing another degree in Mass Communication and also working at the state radio station. Every night, Mi and I would sit outside close to a kiosk and talk about politics, relationship and music. Mi had an uncanny way of talking about music. Whenever my girlfriend called, she would speak to her and ask her to pay her for taking care of her husband. It was always amusing to hear her say that but Mi was free spirited and exude the energy of someone that was always cheerful.

I received all calls that came whenever I was with Mi in her presence but Mi received most of her calls moving away from ear shot, she would move away from me to a place where I couldn't hear the conversation. I was very comfortable with that. I've always understood that privacy and boundaries were central to human relationships. Whenever Mi returned from her calls, we would simply continue from the point of our conversation.

The toll of the virus continued to rise, the world was feeling the heat, and death continued to claim people through COVID-19. Nasarawa had recorded its victim and trepidation, caution and reckless abandon were still in existence. One night, I was sitting outside with Mi and we were talking about some of the lessons that we learned from the pandemic. Mi said that this has taught her that life is fickle and unpredictable. I thought that was a grand thing to say and I wanted her to explain what she meant.. Life is fickle, it is continuously changing and when it does it replaces problems either with a bigger version or with a smaller one, "Problem no dey finish," she said. I understood that to be the quote of the year because everywhere you go, everyone was either quoting it, "Problem no dey finish, enjoy your life o," or simply quoting a similar version.

Mi wanted to know how I feel about this pandemic and I told her that I feel strongly that it stole my plans from me. I had hoped that I would have completed the first part of my degree and gearing up towards next year to complete the final lap.

I was talking about how I had to retweak my plans when Mi took a brief excuse to receive a call. I saw her walk hurriedly to a dark, far place. When Mi came back, she was crying. I was mortified. I have never seen Mi cry. Mi was crying because she had just confirmed that her boyfriend was married for four years and this had deeply torn her apart. Like everything that happened in 2020, it was obvious that this news was totally unexpected. I felt extremely sad for her and I tried to cheer her up but I was making very little progress. Mi said she was going to sleep at her female friend's apartment. It was 9pm, and I walked her to the place.

OF HIGHS AND LOWS
Tobi Eyinade

I leapt into his arms like I typically do at the departure hall of Nnamdi Azikiwe International Airport, Abuja. I lingered in his embrace for longer than usual, not wanting to let go, as if it were my last. Thank God it wasn't but it almost felt like eternity till the universe would present me with an opportunity to do that again. This was in mid-March 2020, before the fast spreading COVID-19 made its entry in Nigeria.

"Only white people test positive for the novel coronavirus. Black/coloured people are immune to the virus," It was easy to hear people say this until Idris Elba tested positive. 67,960 new cases confirmed. Suspension of local and international flights operation announced. Nationwide lockdown announced. And the many news that herald the state of inactivity kept coming.

As if to add salt to the wound that is 2020, there were several other deaths of notable individuals. It all felt like a far echoing case of bad news for me until the demise of my dear friend and colleague brought it home. The finality of my friend's death personally makes 2020 a year I will not forget in a hurry. It seems like the year wasn't going to give anyone a break and just when we are about to catch our breath, another unimaginable event happens.

In spite of all of these, there were some elements of good in this epic year. I took some giant leaps, and made some major milestones. Which brings me to my first lesson in 2020. That it is in a black pot that the purest and whitest of pap is made. That in the midst of upheavals, beauty can be unleashed.

God has a great sense of humour. At our expense, he must have had a good laugh at us as vision boards were made nonsense, planners and diaries were rendered useless at the face of the most unexpected turn of events. It's interesting how the subject of vision boarding trended during the transition weeks between 2019-2020. If you didn't attend a vision board party, you are not ready to conquer the year. Until lady Rona showed up and humbled us and brought us to our lowest form of humanity. The reins of control were literally taken off me and I had to come to a place of beautiful surrender. This year, I was vulnerable.

Business wise, lean, agile and cash flow and a few other business concepts took a new meaning to me. I made decisions on my toes. There was little or no room for "analysis paralysis." I just moved on every idea at the speed of light. The enormous responsibility of being a source of livelihood for many breadwinners made me snap out of the early anxiety the lockdown came with.

I was impressed at my novelty and capacity to build a system and make it work for the team. My business became more than just a book sales venture. Most part of the lockdown, I became more aware of how much of a conduit of hope, knowledge and transformation I can be to many, both far and near. Our stores by sheer demand remained open, our revenue enjoyed a drastic increase and our reach grew tremendously.

In 2020, I fell in love with myself anew and enjoyed my company. I am particularly thankful for the gift of abundant *me times*.

Rest, the word for the year at Daystar couldn't have been more potent as I unabashedly embraced it. I practiced mindfulness this year. Appreciated the little things and became more confident in my own journey.

The year 2020 sure shocked and shifted me at my core. However, I am grateful for the opportunities it presented, the dire lessons I learnt and the true meaning of trust and gratitude, I came to know.

A LOCKDOWN HERO
Albarka Wakili

One of the perks of anticipating the end of life is the way it makes you value things you once took for granted. First time you heard about COVID-19, you laughed it off, you assumed it was just another form of influenza that would have little effect on your life. In a remarkably short time, it was the only subject in town. You were caught by surprise. Your life suddenly and profoundly changed within the space of days.

You started off the year auspiciously. You had a wonderful family time in January. Your elder brother flew out of the country in February. He assured you, in confidence that you were also going to leave home soon. Your ex-girlfriend texted that she was finding it impossible to move on. Everything was moving smoothly until a few hours before your birthday in March.

Around 11PM, you received a notification on your phone. It was one of those 'We regret to inform you that your application has been declined' emails. You became overly distraught. You took your devastated self to sleep hoping that birthday messages from people would revitalize your energy to rise again. When you woke up, your phone which was super active and fully charged wouldn't switch on due to some operating systems defaults. You couldn't view, respond, nor reply to your friends. You went MIA on your big day. No communication, no explanations. Only left with the knowledge that bandwidths of good wishes were floating in the virtual spaces, but you couldn't see them. That day, you felt as though you were at a living funeral receiving flowers you could no longer smell. You would spend the next five months, lockdown period without a phone.

March ending, the government announced the compulsory lockdown of every sector of life. Airports shutdown, religious gatherings postponed, schools shutdown. Your student friends had to come back home. You started receiving updates from NCDC, numbers kept going up like streams from a newly released hit song. As the numbers went up, so did your panic and anxiety.

Beginning of the lockdown, you were out with your friends exchanging your plight about how challenging, stretching, sobering and ultimately boring the lockdown was becoming. You all talked of an idea of a routine exercise every morning since there was no recorded case in your town yet. A friend suggested you rather get a football to play. Another friend volunteered to buy the ball. By the next week, a camaraderie football team was formed. You all agreed to call the team "Lockdown Heroes".

Weeks passed, you invited your friends over to play FIFA19 on PS. You were all keen on forgetting the severity of the damages caused by the virus so you play tournaments. Your friends came every day to spend more than half a day at your place. Then June came and everything got tighter. Lockdown rules got stricter. Relatable economic hardship became visible and evident in your daily discourse as you named your FIFA tournaments numerically. Before you realized, you were on your "Lockdown: 21st Tournament". Nobody cared about who won anymore. You just played to erode the anxiety that ate you up every day. Then one day, it was announced that the Chief of Staff, Abba Kyari died of the virus. More paranoia was sent in the air. You began to be more careful about every contact you made. Began to be uncomfortable about even your friends' visit. Or maybe you were just scared that this might be the beginning of the end of days. Especially after they registered 3 new cases of the virus in your state that same week.

Another day came, then another. One day, your only device of catching fun also caught a cold, gave up the ghost and crashed. Your PS overheated, even the console wore out and there was nobody to console you. That was when you felt the last straw. The loneliness. When you got pushed to the wall. When you realized there were no more options to compromise but to fight back. Fight back the boredom, anxiety and depression that enveloped you. You lost faith, then regained it. You tried to understand God's ways more, His grace, His providence, His favour. And even His silence, especially in that turbulent time. Or maybe God wasn't completely silent. Maybe he responded in tones of rainfall, morsels of food, in every single breath but you were too distracted by the rising number of cases to notice. Or maybe somehow, you found the eloquent silence comforting.

You lost the track of time hoping time doesn't lose track of you. You resorted to finding new things to do. New legal things to do. New spiritual practices. Binging movies, timing yourself to finish a book every week. Now you can proudly say that African Writers Series has got nothing on you. You learned chess. You also wowed your friends when you hit premium on scrabble. Just appreciating the simple things of life. Now you have received the gift of time in which to slow down and contemplate. You are reminded that there is a time for everything in life. You seek for divine companionship to look at each day as a new opportunity to be more compassionate, hospitable and loving.

***

To those of us who lost loved ones this year, may the deceased find repose in the bosom of the divine. To those of us who are still grappling with the complexities of the times, we are not waiting on things to go back to normal but to reimagine how transformed we will be by the changes happening.

So much depends on digging deep into our souls to find the spark of hope and creativity. Such strategies only occur to us in times of adversity, when our usual glide through routine conformity is disrupted. And as we continue to overcome, just like some of us overcame, we are all Lockdown Heroes.

COVID-19 AND ME
Zainab Muhammed

The world was used to running. It appeared that every single person on earth thought it impossible to not continually be in motion. Since the clock was always ticking, time was worshipped. I thought the world would stop if we all stopped moving. If we all thought the earth moved around its orbit because we never stopped running, then COVID-19 came.

Earth experienced a change it didn't see coming. I still wonder why movies that showed us 2030 didn't tell us how 2020 would be. COVID-19 introduced us to a system we didn't think we'd completely depend on. It is true that we were used to virtual meetings, but we didn't think that a time would come when we'd only be able to meet virtually.

COVID-19 has proved that not everyone needs to be at the office to get work done. It has also proved that nothing is too important. We discovered that more than time, life is more important. We found that businesses could wait. Parties, meetings, and everything that kept us on our feet could wait.

The wait made us suffer losses. Countries ran into recession. But I wouldn't say the effect of COVID-19 has been completely negative. I haven't forgotten that lives were lost, I also haven't forgotten that a lot of people were severely depressed. Our loss breaks my heart. But I am one of the few who are on one hand sad about COVID-19's negative effect and on the other hand bold enough to say that it wasn't all that bad.

Time spent at home gave me a chance to discover myself. And yes, I'm not only thankful that I survived, but I'm also thankful that I found myself. I discovered that writing is all I want to do. Do not assume that isolation was a reason I began to spill ink, because it really wasn't. I started writing before the pandemic. But did I know writing is all I want? No. Did I know writing for my blog would awaken the sleeping writer in me? By now you must have caught up with the fact that I started a blog during the pandemic.

If you look for me now, you'd first find that I'm a writer, but this writer studies Biochemistry. And time spent in classes and laboratories refuses to give space for the writer in me to surface. I knew I'd appreciate time off school; COVID-19 gave that. Time spent in isolation put my mind to work. I saw myself create stories, and I saw my hands eager to show my readers the thoughts in my head.

I can say now that before the break, I was following a laid down pattern– school, tests, classes... But I wouldn't admit to myself that I was doing all that for the sake of it. When I saw the poems I wrote, I saw myself smile. There were times I read my blog posts and was marvelled at them. The beauty of combining words, was what kept me entertained through the moment of pain. The moment when we saw figures showing the increasing departure of people we don't know, and for some, people they knew.

ONLY WHEN YOU SPEAK UP
Osatare Omonkhegbe

When I welcomed the new year, I was a 22-year old medical student enthusiastic to continue her fourth year. Armed with my new year resolutions, I was ready to take on the first year of a new decade. I was ready to make better decisions in my life so I wouldn't mess up the new opportunity I'd been given.

Little did I know that all those plans would disintegrate into dust, through no fault of mine but by forces beyond my control, forces I'd failed to take into consideration in my planning. But you can't blame me because nobody predicted this.

I have never before experienced as many emotions as I did this year. So many highs and lows. Nevertheless, I have learned a lot too. I have made some startling discoveries about myself, my family, and even my country.

The lockdown period allowed me to spend a lot of time with my family, more time than I would have liked but thinking about it now, I realize that I wouldn't have had it any other way. You see, I have learned that family is one of life's greatest treasures and one you would love to have close when life smiles on you and even when it decides to throw lemons at you. My mental health was highly preserved because I was surrounded by love. It's truly the best place to be.

Soon enough I started to get restless because I knew that I couldn't afford to waste this opportunity. Being a medical student, I hardly have any free time. I had already had a glimpse at the unpredictability of life, so I had to start. I just had to start. The resolutions I had written at the beginning of the year couldn't lie fallow just because everything had gone awry. I decided to do the best I could with what I had been given. Time. So I started writing again, I started exercising again, I started trying new recipes in the kitchen. I started praying and studying my Bible again, I was determined to know God for myself, to practice faith instead of religion. I didn't want to remain the same at the end, I had to make myself believe that there would be an end. I even read a self-help book. I hate self-help books but this one turned out to be really informative. It taught me how to better manage my finances. All of these practices kept me sane even when the terror felt endless.

Apart from the pandemic raging around us, new threats came in the form of police brutality. It felt good to see the uprising, the movement that began all over the world against this injustice. This ongoing battle has made me understand that only when you speak up and demand freedom will you be paid any attention. If you keep bearing the pains of injustice in silence, hoping in silence for change, praying in silence, nothing will come of it.

The crimes against women also shook me. It is sad that as a female, living in this world means I have to constantly fight for my survival. I have to fight the unjust government, fight the philosophy that there should be limits to my thoughts and deeds, I have to fight the people around me for my right to freely live. It is sad, indeed but I'm glad we didn't stay quiet, instead we showed our strength to those who doubted us in the first place.

I have learned so much from this whirlwind roller coaster ride called 2020 but the one thing I have inscribed in my heart is to live, not just exist. Focus on what's important while enjoying life as much as possible. Don't put off your aspirations and dreams. Start as soon as possible because the end will come and when it does, you don't want to leave behind a load of 'what-ifs' and 'shouldas'.

When I welcomed the new year, I was a 22-year old medical student enthusiastic to continue her fourth year. Nevertheless, I will be leaving this year, a 23-year old medical student still in her fourth year but with a new look in her eyes and a mantra in her lips pushing her towards a bigger goal because this battle called life has to count for something for her, for her family and for her country.

HIGH HOPES
Oluwabukunmi Familoye

2020 started on a great note for me. Hopes were high. It was time to achieve the Vision-2020 as we had conceived it since we were kids. Little did we know what is to come and then, days into February, news of a ravaging virus began to trend.

When the outbreak started in 2019, I knew it was a matter of time before it came into Nigeria. It was a scary thought but it was realistic. As a pharmacist, I knew that unlike the developed countries like the United States, we do not have the necessary health infrastructure to combat this virus. So, it felt like an impending doom waiting to happen.

In the typical Nigerian reaction to impending danger, we tried to pray it away and wish it away because we think we are God's favourite people. Unfortunately, God has no favourites. We left our doors open and the virus finally got to us. Although the virus itself might not have taken so many lives, the spiral effect of the lockdown on the economy was bad for us.

My premonitions and speculations did not prepare me for the experience that followed. The fear, the confusion, and the uncertainties. It felt like the end of the world. Words like 'Shutdown', 'Work from home', 'new normal' became the buzzword all over.

One of the greatest lessons I learned during this period is there is no new thing under the sun. Whatever was happening to us had happened to people years before. History is a map filled with events, we go to it to learn about past mistakes, and then we go to it to find a path that leads to a better future. There are patterns everywhere, we just have to look closely, pay some more attention and COVID-19 or Coronavirus pandemic was another play out of the 1918 influenza virus. Only this time, the world is more advanced with regard to science and technology, which to me was a great advantage. I spent time researching, reading journals, and articles. I learned to listen to unsaid words and interpret data correctly beyond what mainstream media wanted us to believe.

Also, the shutdown as a result of the pandemic helped me reflect on the things that are most important in life — People (family, friends). I think most of us realized that we need each other to survive. We found solace in people who love us and whom we loved in return.

2020 also reminds me of how fallible humans and human systems are. Even the so-called best systems can crumble when the storm comes. There is really no perfect system or governance anywhere even though some are more advanced than others. We also witnessed massive ignorance of some leaders (religious and political). I was reminded that the leaders we hold in high esteem are just men too subject to flaws and errors.

I learned that there are things outside our control and there is really nothing we can do about them.

I think the pandemic and all that happened created a chain of events that led to the protests against police brutality in Nigeria and the United States. We had time to reflect on our journey as a nation and we realized that we were doing poorly. The protest was needed for a rebirth especially for the millennials and Gen Z who had been born into a failing country. I never would have thought that I would take part in a national protest prior to this time. But I did. I learned the power of oneness of mind, spirit, and voice.

Finally, I think 2020 is just like every other year. Full of evils, darkness, and bad occurrences, only this time it affected everyone on a large scale.

The bottom line is this: learn to love wholly, give more, and live fully. Do not wait till a pandemic forces you to take periodic reflections on the things that matter to you. Always take a break in between all of your journeys in this fast-paced world and re-evaluate the things that matter to you.

Some things are out of your control, do not fight them. Do not pressure yourself unnecessarily. Being alive is one thing to be grateful for.

NO ONE KNOWS
R'Jay

Just like every other person, I was really looking forward to 2020. I just had this strong conviction that 2020 was going to be my year, and I would do great things in the year.

Normally, I come up with my goals for the new year during the last week of the previous year but for some weird reasons, I didn't come up with goals at the end of 2019. Nothing seemed to be coming to my head, it felt really clumsy and I thought I would be able to write the goals at the beginning of the new year. Lo and behold, the new year came, and I found myself struggling, partly because I was still trying to adjust to a new job I started in October 2019.

Fast forward to February 2020, things started to pick up. I wrote my goals, I was beginning to do well in my job, I work as a Media Marketing Executive in a radio station in Lagos, and for a newbie in media marketing, I was already doing well as of February 2020.

The grass was looking very very green in March, and all of a sudden, the pandemic struck and the green grass all of a sudden started to turn yellow.

While fear gripped the whole world, the reverse was the case for me because I was daily connected to service. During that period, we had special online programmes daily, we prayed, we fasted, we broke bread, we strengthened ourselves in God, and like never before, there was a fresh hunger to win souls. Spiritually, this pandemic threw me even closer to God.

2020 made me value and appreciate the people in my life the more. Going months without seeing friends and family was not easy. You needed to see how I hugged my friends when I finally got to see them after the lockdown was relaxed. The whole lockdown made me realize how fickle life is, and how things can change at any given time. Most times, we take our loved ones for granted, or better still, we 'see them finish' forgetting how important these people are to us. 2020 reawakened the love we have for one another and value all the memories we have together, as friends and family.

I have been working for about 3 years now, and if there is one year that was the most challenging in my career, it had to be 2020. Like I mentioned in the previous paragraphs, I delved into the Media Marketing world in October 2019, and I was just picking up when the pandemic struck in March. As a Media Marketer, my job, in summary, is to bring adverts to the station, so you can imagine how difficult my job was owing to the fact that a lot of companies made huge losses while some shut down totally.

When things started picking up, and we were making little sales, another curfew was imposed on Lagos state as a result of the End SARS protest. It was a rollercoaster experience but the fact that I didn't lose my job was something to be grateful for.

Talking about the protest, that period was quite draining. I had to shut down social media for a few days to maintain my sanity. I cried and prayed a lot. How the protest went from a peaceful one to the death of innocent youths was devastating. The hate on social media, the false news, the intimidation, just name it, was a whole lot.

Of course, the financial aspect of 2020 can't be neglected! Thank God I didn't lose my job but just like other companies, a part of our salary had to go to help keep the station running. Initially, I didn't feel the cut considering there was a lockdown so there was nothing much to spend money on but when work resumed fully, I started to feel the impact. But again, the fact that I had more than one source of income actually helped. I was still able to save some money. I told myself, I'd not let a month go by without saving, and trust me, it is one of the best financial decisions that I have made. One lesson I learnt in 2020 in terms of finances is, as much as possible, don't rely on just one source of income.

On the flip side, the lockdown actually came with clarity. It was during the lockdown that I niched down, creating only relationship-related content for my Instagram audience, and I also started my YouTube channel, something I'd been postponing for years. I met lots of amazing people on social media too.

If 'nobody knows tomorrow' or 'never say never' was a year, it would have been 2020. Nobody ever thought there would come a time where the whole world would be on lockdown but guess what, it happened in 2020. A lot of people that planned to travel this year didn't know that would be anything like COVID-19 to disrupt their plans. As a matter of fact, I got an all-expense paid trip to the US in July but could not make it because of the pandemic, it was painful but the fact that I am alive and healthy is really soothing and something to be grateful for about.

I told myself that I'm not going to put pressure on myself about the goals I was not able to accomplish. I'm channelling all my energy into thanking God for good health and life, and I think you should do the same too. Instead of focusing on the losses, count your blessings!

DEAR DIARY
Eniola Oluwafolakemi Olatoye

Dear diary,

Today, my cousin, Ellie said that the year of our Lord, two thousand and twenty has so far felt like seven years compressed into one, and with its wealth of content and the experiences we have had, I most definitely agree.

Today included my typical sleep-wake-eat-read-netflix routine, which I won't bore you with. But that wasn't all. I am currently watching Kal Ho Naa Ho, I'm guessing you know what that means... I wrote another condolence letter today, from my office, the council, to the student body. Another young promising person left the world too early.

It has felt like too many people have gone this year, that is, beyond the fair number of deaths, a year should have. But then, in years to come, death will still be a part of life. And maybe there is something to learn from all these losses hitting left and right this year. After receiving all the bad news, I decided to watch Kal Ho Naa Ho because I get to laugh at the comedy, giggle and blush at the lovey-dovey parts. I ended up crying at the end when Aman (Shah Rukh

Khan) died. The theme song translates as, "live every moment to the fullest...for tomorrow may never come".

We never really want to think about death. We want to be assured that we will wake up tomorrow and go to sleep every day, peacefully, till we're very old. But if indeed you get tomorrow, what assures you that your neighbour gets tomorrow too?

The uncertainty of this year has helped me accept that we really do not know who is and isn't going to be here tomorrow. So why not do what's possible today? Why wait? And I am learning to apply this in my relationship with people. My biggest regret this year is not insisting to my parents on traveling to visit my aunt and attend the naming ceremony of my newest cousin. We just assumed, as we usually do, there'll be another day to visit, and my aunt passed on ten days after the naming ceremony. That's it! I'm never seeing her again.

So, if I can visit that friend today, why wait? If their dress is lovely today, why not give that compliment? Why not crack that joke and make them laugh? Why not buy that present for no reason? Why not pay their cab fare? It's these little things we'll remember and hold on to tomorrow. When they're gone, I'll be happy I once made their day. Or when I'm gone, they'll be glad I touched them.

Let me talk a little about this morning. We were eating breakfast and my Uncle Sunny just decided it would be a nice time to put us on hot seats, asking about our career choices and what informed these choices. It felt odd at first, being that adults would usually assume we'd practice what we're studying. To get out of the discussion, I considered either fainting or choking on my yam, but I'm not a great actress, so I just answered the question instead. And oh, the breath of fresh air that went through my lungs when he didn't seem disappointed that I had not yet decided. He talked about the state of the world right now and how we must bear it all in mind to understand what kind of value we actually need to offer the world.

Before now, I have already observed that brands are no longer marketing commodities and services, but instead market feelings, like joy and self-confidence. Marketing strategies rely heavily on how you feel when you use the products. And today it made more sense. There's so much negativity and everyone is just finding means to escape reality to the extent that everything that will appeal to you in these times must feel like an escape route. But it's all just ephemeral. The world needs value. And whatever it is I end up choosing, of the various career options I'm considering, I have learnt today that positive change must be made and real value must be added. And even at a time like this in our country, with the #EndSARS movement, humanitarian concerns, and human rights consciousness, most young adults in this country have taken up the challenge for greatness and I'm happy to see. And this sense of consciousness is going with me into whatever career path. I've learnt that there's too much to be fixed and to be done.

Before the Netflix part of my routine today, I read an article online and the whole point of the article took me back to Starr's (Amandla Steinberg) words on The Hate U Give, where she said "if you don't see my black, you don't see me". The writer of the article, a black American woman, was simply talking about how being "colour-blind" is not exactly how to learn to accept people or how to end racism. And that's a lesson I find very useful in these times, particularly here in Nigeria. The events of the past month have got us talking about putting an end to profiling. And now, more conversations are coming up due to the truckload of issues we actually have around here, bordering around something like getting rid of "state of origin" from forms to help foster a sense of unity, and also to erase favouritism to an extent. While this can help, I can't help but wonder if I really want a part of my identity ignored for me to be accepted or loved. Does that lady with the tattoos necessarily want you to pretend like you can't see them? Does that young man want you to ignore his place of origin so you don't mistake him for a terrorist rather than the victim he is? A lot of things shape who we are, among which are identity, experiences, and choices. And we do not necessarily have to be blind to any one of these for a person to be more acceptable in our sight, or for a person to not be unduly favoured.

As a Christian and as a person who cares about my interpersonal relationships, I wonder if it is really love if I can't let myself see a person fully for who they really are to be able to accept them. And so, I'm challenging myself to learn to love and be fully accepting without any form of partial blindness.

Well, I guess I can say today has been another day of lessons in the year of our Lord, Two thousand and twenty.

Till tomorrow, Diary.

Xoxo.

CONTRIBUTORS' NOTE

ALBARKA WAKILI is a prolific rapper, writer and performing artist from Jalingo, Nigeria. He is a graduate of English and Media studies (Hons) from Africa University, Zimbabwe. He won the Best Nigerian Student Award and the prestigious Machakanja Family Awards in Linguistics in 2018. You can connect with him on Twitter and Instagram as @wakillz

AVWEMOYA IZODUWA OGHENEOCHUKO. Writer.

BASIT JAMIU is the Founding Editor of AfroAnthology Series. His works have appeared in African Writer, Brittle Paper, Afri Diaspora, Kalahari Review, Saraba Magazine, Praxis Magazine Online, Expound Magazine and many other platforms. In 2018, he was the recipient of YNaija's New Establishment list for his work at AfroAnthology. He has been described as among the "top curators and editors from Africa". He tweets @CuratorBasit and watches TV Series among other fun activities.

BUSAYO OYEWOLE is a writer and product designer living in Berlin. She's the host of The One

Question podcast, where she asks her guests just one question. She tweets at @busayyo

ENIOLA OLUWAFOLAKEMI OLATOYE is a student of the Faculty of Law, University of Ibadan. She runs her own blog, Olúwáfọláké̩mi Unfiltered. And she is currently serving as the Clerk (a principal officer) of the Students' Representative Council, UI.

HANEEFAH ABDULRAHMAN is an interviewer, a writer, a spoken poetry artiste and a podcaster. Born in Kaduna, Haneefah is an indigene of Kogi. She is the 2020 financial secretary and Editor of the Creative Writers Club, Ahmadu Bello University, Zaria and the assistant editor of Literature Voices, she was selected as a delegate for the Conference Leadership Training of A.B.U for all ENACTUS schools in Nigeria which qualified her as a Project Head. She is a very active member of Hilltop Creative Arts Foundation and many other literary platforms. She has published in Daily Trust, Nigerian Review as well as many other journals.

IBRAHIM BABÁTÚNDÉ IBRAHIM. After he was forcibly sent to science-class in high-school, it took Ibrahim 20 years to finally find his way back to his passion, in 2019, when he left a successful ten-year career in media & entertainment to become a writer. In that time, his works have appeared in Door is a Jar Magazine, Ake Review, Agbowó Magazine, Black Muslim Reads Anthology, Analogies & Allegories Literary Magazine, and more. He finished as a finalist in Goge Africa's #GogeAfrica20 Writing Contest, and Ibua Journal's Packlight Series. He has also been nominated for the Pushcart Prize. Ibrahim's work explores the human experience from an African perspective. He's @heemthewriter across social media.

LAWRETTA EGBA is a professional writer, financial analyst, and communications strategist. She is a Chartered Accountant and has a BSc in Accounting as well as a masters in media and communication with Pan Atlantic University, in view. She has years of experience in investment banking, private equity, and ghostwriting, and has written for a myriad of platforms in Nigeria and the diaspora including Future Africa Forum, Opera News, Nairametrics, The Guardian, Premium Times, and more. Through her company, Cyno Group, she has also written for organizations like Quantum Zenith, Yochaa, Lagos State Ministry of Economic Planning & Budget, FITC, and more. She is a Toastmaster and a brown belt Karateka.

OLUWABUKUNMI FAMILOYE is the Founder of Bookhub Nigeria, an education startup, with the aim of raising intellectual and well-informed leaders by equipping them with knowledge and skills for all round development. She is passionate about increasing the literacy rate in Africa and empowering young people to lead successful lives. Oluwabukunmi holds a Bachelor's degree in Pharmacy from Obafemi Awolowo University, Osun state Nigeria. In addition to her work with Bookhub, she volunteers on different health community projects and startups. She also enjoys explaining complex concepts and ideas which she expresses through her writings on medium. She would love to travel around the world. Her dream is to build well-equipped libraries in low-income communities around Africa.

OSATARE OMONKHEGBE is a medical student of Ambrose Alli University, Edo State, Nigeria. She is a young writer with several short stories and poems to her name and currently runs a blog, Tales by Tare. As a content creator and copywriter, Tare uses the digital space to tell her stories.

R'JAY is a Relationship Enthusiast who is passionate about inspiring millennials to have healthy relationships. She is a Mass Communication graduate from the University of Ilorin. R'Jay is a freelance voice over artist with Addendum media, and works as a Media Executive in a radio station in Lagos. She's also the founder of R'Jay Initiative. A community aimed at reducing menstrual poverty and improving the lives of youths.

TOBI EYINADE is an Abba's girl. She finds her essence in Him and enjoys the simple but beautiful things of life. She is a bringer of joy and a quirky dancer. She delights in cheering others on, likes a good chance at hearty laughter, and loves a heavy dose of quality time with family, nature, books and wine. She is fascinated and inspired by authentic people doing extraordinary things in their everyday lives. Tobi is also passionate about social impact and devising home-grown but innovative solutions to the problem of unemployment, education and poverty in Nigeria. She is the co-founder of Rovingheights and founder of The Book Lady NG.

ZAINAB MUHAMMED, known by her readers as Zaynerb, is a poet, and writer. She writes because words just won't let her be. She lives in Lagos, and studies biochemistry in Ekiti State University. Read her poems @iamzaynerb on Instagram.

Made in the USA
Columbia, SC
02 September 2022